THE LITTLE BOOK OF
SECRETS

D0826981

THE LITTLE BOOK OF
SECRETS

*gentle wisdom for
joyful living*

CHRIS PRENTISS

Power Press
Los Angeles, California

Library of Congress Control Number: 2008931490

Copyright © 2008 by Chris Prentiss. All rights reserved. Printed in the
United States of America. No part of this book may be used or reproduced
in any manner whatsoever without written permission except in the case
of brief quotations embodied in critical articles or reviews.

ISBN: 978-0-943015-58-3

10 9 8 7 6 5 4 3 2 1

For information, address:

Power Press
6428 Meadows Court
Malibu, California 90265
Telephone: 310-392-9393
E-mail: info@PowerPressPublishing.com
Website: www.PowerPressPublishing.com

For foreign and translation rights, contact Nigel J. Yorwerth
E-mail: Nigel@PublishingCoaches.com

Cover design: Roger Gefvert
Interior design: James Bennett

Grateful acknowledgements to Nigel J. Yorwerth and Patricia Spadaro of
Yorwerth Associates/PublishingCoaches.com for their expert packaging,
editing, and guidance of this book through all of its phases.

AUTHOR'S NOTE

I humbly apologize to my women readers for using *he*, *his*, and *him*
in this work. Using *he/she* becomes cumbersome for the reader and
disturbs the flow of thought. I have, therefore, chosen to use the
masculine form to make the reading easy and the wisdom simple
to understand.

For Taylor

PREFACE

"Never tell the truth!" I was three and half, and it was the first of the lessons my mother, Bea, was to teach me over the next twenty years. She said, "Only fools tell the truth." And she followed it up with "Never tell the truth when a good lie will suffice." One of her lessons in lying was "a good liar has to have a good memory." So I memorized endless poems to improve my memory. I was never permitted to call her mom or mother, only Bea.

Bea was born in New York City in 1900. Her father was a longshoreman who worked on the docks, and her mother was a stay-at-home mom, who took care of her and her two sisters and brother. When Bea was fifteen, she was raped by an older man and became pregnant. In those days, it was a time of shotgun weddings and they forced this older man to marry Bea. They hated each other, and Bea said he delighted in tormenting her. She sewed buttons on shirts for fifty cents a day to get spending money. When she got out of the marriage three years later, she was tough and hard.

She was also totally unforgiving, never forgetting a wrongdoing and waiting patiently to pay back a wrong done to her. Her motto was "six times double." That meant she would repay the wrongdoer six times double for the pain he or she had caused her. I saw her wait twenty-four years to repay one man who had wronged her, and the glee and happiness she experienced kept her laughing for months. As for the man who raped her, she caused him endless pain through the years. She spread rumors and lies about him, sporadically ruining his life every few years until she was satisfied he had been repaid six times double.

In the roaring twenties, Bea was in her twenties. She was poor and learned to live by her wits in a wild and lawless element of New York City. She turned to a life of crime. By the time she was twenty-one, she ran the largest stolen car ring in New Jersey and had a gang of con artists working for her in New York City. When prohibition began, Bea was immediately on the scene running whiskey to the speakeasies. She became successful living outside the law and was determined that I, too, should become successful in the same way.

By the time I was four, Bea had taught me shoplifting, and I was praised warmly for my little successes. A single parent, she taught me to survive by any means, and I learned well. My early business career was characterized by deceit, trickery, and fraud. No one was safe. I even cheated my friends. It was great fun and I made some money doing it. In the evening, Bea and I would sit and talk about the cheating and conniving we had done, and we shared many a good laugh over our trickery. Bea also had a wonderful sense of humor, but it was not the usual kind of humor. She would laugh heartily over someone else's misery—not in a mean way, but in a genuinely funny way that was so comical that everyone listening would join in.

Two small stories about Bea will further reveal her character to you. When I was in the sixth grade, my two brothers and I went to a sophisticated private school. It had its own golf course. Toward the end of the school year, my two brothers, who had been less than studious, were in danger of failing. The night before the final exams, Bea climbed the wall surrounding the school, broke into the headmaster's office, stole the final exams, came home and tutored us for several hours, then returned to the school and put the exams back.

The next story was told to me by my father, Ralph Prentice, whom I first met when I was forty-four. He was a writer who made part of his living writing stories for *The Saturday Evening Post*. He and Bea were driving around in one of her beautiful cars when Ralph spotted a magnificent sedan. He exclaimed, "Bea, look at the wonderful car!" She said, "Do you like that car, Ralph? That's a Stutz Bearcat." The next morning there was a Stutz Bearcat parked in Ralph's driveway. He was overwhelmed with gratitude and remembers saying, "Oh, Bea, what a wonderful gift! You shouldn't have done it—it's so expensive." Of course, Bea had stolen the car and she laughed for a whole month while she waited for Ralph to be arrested, which he was. Bea had paid off the police and nothing came of it except a huge joke at Ralph's expense.

One of Bea's many saving graces was her generosity. I've never met anyone as tough and hard but also as courageous, resourceful, and wonderfully giving as Bea. We moved to New Jersey in 1940, one step ahead of the law, and she became a real estate broker and insurance agent. She gave away most of her commissions to help people get started in new homes. She was loved by everyone, except those who managed to get on her bad side, and then she was an implacable enemy.

Because of her generosity, Bea became a bit of a

political force in our small township, controlling enough votes to swing elections. One of her lovers, Carl, a stone mason by trade, wanted to become tax collector and Bea had enough of a following to get him elected. A couple of years later, he wanted to become mayor, and she obliged him by getting him elected by an overwhelming majority. He became very egotistical, jilted Bea, and moved out of our house. When he came up for reelection, Bea contacted just about everyone in town, creating a lie to tell each person. For the veterans, she said Carl hated veterans. For the crippled, she said he hated cripples. You get the idea. He was voted out of office by the same huge majority and was so badly damaged by the lies she spread that he couldn't even get work as a mason. Bea was happy.

She carried a gun until the day she died in 1994. I was holding her hand when she left her body and moved on. The last thing I did was to take her gun from under her pillow.

What saved me from a life of crime was my appetite for reading. I read every day, mostly fiction, and through the books I began to perceive a different way of life. I read of courage, valor, integrity, and a life lived as a hero. I was powerfully drawn to such a life. One day, when I was twenty-five, I sat at my kitchen table and looked around at the shambles I had made of my life. Sure, I had made some money, but I hadn't been able to hold onto any of it. I had no real friends, everyone was afraid of me because I was so deceitful, and my reputation was terrible. I was a failure as a husband, a father, a friend, a businessman—and as a man. I had hurt so many people. I realized that Bea, that warmhearted, generous, fun-loving, protective mother whom I loved and who loved me, had programmed me 180 degrees in the wrong direction. If I continued to follow the course she had set for me, I would surely wind up in prison, friendless and alone.

I was overwhelmed by remorse, and I made a decision to discover the way to real success, real happiness, real love, real inner peace, and lasting prosperity. I tried to turn my life around in New Jersey, but Bea's influence was too strong. So in 1965, I went to California, determined to become the man I dreamed of being. When I told Bea of my purpose, she replied, "What a jerk!" She had nothing but scorn for living that type of life.

I spent the next forty years searching the world for the secrets that have sustained people and brought them true success, prosperity, and lasting happiness. My search has taken me to many lands, and I have read the world's most ancient writings that have been handed down to this day. Those teachings have survived thousands of years because of their immense value to people. In those writings, I discovered a clear path that led to the wonderful gifts I sought.

Following the path of the secrets has brought me and others to whom I have revealed the secrets all the good things we most dearly cherish: true friendship, prosperity, peace, happiness, wonderful relationships with people we love, rewarding professions, and relationships with our children that are loving, truthful, and totally satisfying. And now I have the great good fortune to be able to write about the secrets and share them with you.

I humbly offer you these ancient secrets with my wish for your deep-down, soul-drenching happiness, abundant prosperity, and unconditional love. These secrets will liberate you, protect you, and bring you good fortune.

As for you, Bea, wherever you are, I offer you great thanks for your constant message to me: "You can do it!"

—Chris Prentiss

THE
SECRETS

*A situation only
becomes favorable
after one adapts to it.*

As long as you are angry, upset, or feel hurt over an event or situation, you will be unable to perceive its beneficial aspects, and you may wear yourself out with unnecessary resistance. The event or situation may have been to your complete advantage from the first moment. Even happy turns of fortune sometimes come to you in a form that seems strange or unlucky. The event itself is simply an event, and the situation is just the setting in which you find yourself. The way you respond to the event or situation is what determines its final outcome in your life. Since you cannot alter the past, once an event has taken place or a situation has been revealed to you, all that is left to you, without exception, is your response. By responding as though what happened was completely for your benefit, you will immediately experience good feelings about what happened; and by acting in accord with your feelings, you will naturally bring about that end as a result of the Universal law of cause and effect. Those who know this one secret and act accordingly will not only be masters of their fate, speeding quickly to the achievement of their goals, but will also enjoy a lifetime of heartwarming happiness and abundant success.

By manifesting a modest attitude,
people will naturally want to help
you and give you good counsel.

It is part of human nature to love and help the modest and to resent and thwart the arrogant. People soon give up helping or counseling an egotistical person who thinks he knows everything. When you are modest, people do not resent you and, consequently, you do not incur opposition. Attaining your goals becomes easy and you readily attract helpers. Because we like to tell others of our accomplishments and talents, it is sometimes difficult to be modest, but the rewards of modesty are far greater than the pleasures of telling of our accomplishments and talents. Practicing this one secret will do more for your success than five years of hard work, and your success will soar as high as the great redwood trees.

Do not hate.
Hatred binds you
to the hated object.

The Universe is favorably inclined. That is how and why it continues. That means that there is more goodness than evil in the world. Hatred is a product of evil. To the extent that you allow yourself to feel hatred, you become an instrument of evil. When you hate someone, your strong emotion draws that person to you. Is that what you want? To eliminate the connection, simply dismiss the person from your thoughts. Consciously stop thinking about that person and replace your thoughts about that person with other thoughts. You may have to do that many times before thoughts of the person stop recurring in your mind, but be assured that eventually those thoughts will stop and you will then be free from the tyranny of your hatred. To combat evil, respond with goodness. Evil cannot exist where goodness thrives.

SECRET 4

Take not gain or loss to heart.
What man holds high
comes to nothing.

You are not your gain; neither are you your loss. Gains and losses are external to you, things with which your eternal soul is not concerned. All gains and losses pass away at the time of death. Do not waste even a moment on gains and losses when death is plucking at your ears saying, "Live! For I am coming."

*In general, opposition appears as
an obstruction, but the knowledgeable
person sees it as an opportunity
and uses it to his advantage.*

Adversity is for your strengthening. A person of true understanding takes each ounce of adversity and turns it to his advantage. Upon encountering opposition, the inferior person, ignorant of the laws of the Universe, bewails his fate, blames others or circumstances, and quits his efforts. The wise person, knowledgeable in the laws of the Universe, uses the opposition to gather strength, improve himself, and take a more beneficial course of action. He sees the opposition as an opportunity and seeks the cause of the opposition within himself. Through this introspection, the external opposition becomes an occasion of inner enrichment and education. By adopting this attitude regarding opposition, your strength will grow as a young bear's, and you will reach your goals as though on the back of Pegasus himself, the fabled winged horse.

Passion and reason
cannot exist side by side.

When anger, lust, hatred, or love consumes you, clear, rational thinking is impossible. Such occasions cause great turmoil in your mind, turmoil that may take many hours and even days to subside. It is only when you are able to calmly step back from yourself and "look in" on yourself that true detachment is achieved. That detachment then permits rational thinking. When you achieve that goal, you make no mistakes.

SECRET 7

In times of prosperity,
it is important to possess enough
greatness of spirit to bear
with the mistakes
of others.

Just as water washes everything clean, the wisest person pardons mistakes and even forgives intentional transgressions. In that way, he insures the upward spiral of his prosperity. The inferior person cannot resist the opportunity to chastise or criticize another and, in so doing, brings resentment onto himself, destroys unanimity, and crushes enthusiasm, thereby destroying his own chances for success. When your star is on the rise, you need only keep your eyes fixed upon it, forgiving all mistakes and transgressions, and you will be drawn to the heights of success as a large kite in a strong wind.

When entangled in a conflict,
it is wise to remain so clearheaded
and strong that you are always
ready to come to terms with
your opponent by meeting
him halfway.

In times of conflict, you are always in danger because your opponent is seeking to harm or take advantage of you. Taking an opportunity to end the conflict by meeting your opponents halfway, or even more than halfway, leads away from a time of danger to a time of security. That is a wise and sensible course of action, and the knowledgeable, successful person seizes the opportunity, knowing that, in truth, he has won a great victory. To carry on a conflict to the bitter end has evil effects since the enmity will continue even if the conflict is won.

If you want to know what anyone is like, you have only to observe what he bestows his care on and what sides of his own nature he cultivates and nourishes.

Each person reveals himself by what he says and does, by the way he dresses, by the ways he responds to events, by what he reads and watches, by the way he stands, by how he is regarded by his friends and associates, and, generally, by the way he lives life. By observing anyone, you can see what that person is like.

*Boasting of your wealth,
position, promotion, success,
or influential friends inevitably
invites misfortune and
humiliation.*

Boasting confirms that you feel inferior, inadequate, and insecure. You are trying to add to your stature by your boasting. It also displays a great lack of understanding of human nature, for we all universally dislike the braggart. The knowledgeable person considers that what he has is sufficient and lets it speak for itself. He acts modestly, and in that way assures his continued success, for the world loves a modest person.

The way of the happy, successful person is to be joyous of heart, yet concerned in thought.

The happy, successful person is concerned in thought because he knows that all periods of prosperity are followed by times of decline and all people are not as they should be. He therefore takes thought for the future and exercises caution in his dealings with people. Nonetheless, no matter how concerned in thought he is, nor how weighty those thoughts may be, his concerns are never enough to dim his inner joy because, above all, he remains aware that he is an indestructible child of a golden Universe.

SECRET 12

To a person of true understanding, it makes no difference whether death comes early or late.

You may have forgotten how you came to Planet Earth, but you do know the way to get here; that is evident. What you have done once, you can probably do again. When you come to know that you *are* the Universe, as much a part of it as the stars, the mountains, and the great galaxies that wheel in space, and that the Universe is eternal, you will realize that you, too, are eternal. Use whatever time you have while you're here to cultivate yourself and use the time productively. Your sense of the ending of life should not impel you to uninhibited revelry in order to enjoy life while it lasts, nor to yield to melancholy and sadness, thereby spoiling the time remaining to you. Knowing that time is only an illusion, you should feel no break with time. Understanding this, you need have no fear of the moment of death, which is only a point of transition. It is like walking through a doorway from one room into another and no more remarkable than any other moment in time.

For power to be truly great,
it must remain united with the
fundamental principles
of right and justice.

The inferior person, concerned only for his own well-being and pleasure, uses his power to further his own selfish ends and to cause hurt and trouble for others. This is the degenerative use of power and bodes ill for everyone, particularly the wielder of the power. The knowledgeable person, concerned with the principles of right and justice, uses his power to aid others and improve the general welfare. This bodes well for everyone, particularly the wielder of the power.

When you see good, you should imitate it. If you have faults, you should rid yourself of them.

J ust as being in the presence of certain people can pull you down, being in the company of well-intentioned people can have a wonderfully beneficial effect upon you, particularly if you take advantage of the opportunity to improve yourself. That ethical attitude is the most important character attribute you can cultivate. It is one of the ways the knowledgeable, successful person brightens his already bright virtue. For persevering in that effort, even among those considered lucky, you will stand out as the chosen one.

*In the hands
of a great master,
all material is useful.*

A great master can find a use for everything and everyone, and he is good at salvage. He wastes nothing; therefore, he always has enough. He values everyone; therefore everyone values him.

*Pleasant manners
succeed even with
irritable people.*

If you do not allow the irritability of others to affect your own pleasant conduct, your pleasant conduct will then influence them. By treating others well, you cause others to treat you well in turn. Because of your thoughtfulness and courtesy, you will gain the respect of others. For prevailing in this secret, your friends and associates will grow as sunflowers after a warm summer rain.

It is wise and reasonable not to try to obtain anything by force.

That which is obtained by force must be held by force. That constant exertion drains your energy, invites the censure of others, and inevitably leads to regret. It is a law of the Universe that what you obtain by force will ultimately bring you misfortune in one form or another, and a knowledgeable, successful person will have none of it. While it may appear that something obtained by force is a temporary benefit to the person who obtained it, in the end, the law will be fulfilled.

*Conflict within
weakens the power to
conquer danger without.*

When the time for action has come, inner conflict will cause you to hesitate. Conflict within a group will prevent members of the group from acting as a unit. In either case, conflict weakens. Great or dangerous undertakings are to be avoided in times of conflict because achieving success requires a concerted unity of force. Making certain that there is no inner conflict when the time for action is at hand will find you ever victorious.

*The small-minded person
is not ashamed of unkindness
and does not shrink
from injustice.*

The inferior, unknowledgeable person is unconcerned with unfairness or unkindness. As a result of natural law, he suffers and does not know that he is the cause of his suffering. The successful person feels diminished by acts of unkindness or injustice, whether they are committed by himself or another. As a result of natural law, he enjoys a life of great good fortune and contentment. He is highly regarded by friends and close associates, is looked up to by all, and easily walks the path that leads to success.

*It is better to
go on foot than ride
in a carriage under
false pretenses.*

It is better to go honorably on foot and do without than to ride in a fine carriage under false pretenses and thereby lose your honor. If you pretend abundance when you are in need, those who would aid you will not because either they will believe you to be abundant or they will recognize your pretense and consider you to be unworthy. Furthermore, by pretending you have something when you do not, you diminish yourself in your own eyes and so lose self-respect. "Who you think you are" is who you are.

To be a knowledgeable, successful person, you should acquaint yourself with many sayings of antiquity and many deeds of the past and thereby strengthen your character.

Character is what determines all your actions and thoughts. In turn, your actions and thoughts determine your future. By studying the sayings that have survived the test of the centuries, you will gain wisdom. By learning of the deeds of your ancient heroes, you will gain inspiration. Wisdom coupled with inspiration leads to great good fortune and supreme success. That is a Universal law.

Once you have gained
inner mastery of a problem,
it will come about naturally
that the action you take
will succeed.

Gaining inner mastery of a problem begins with recognizing that the problem is only in your life because it holds a gift for you. It presents you with an opportunity for improving yourself or your situation. Keep in mind that the solution will put you in better circumstances than before the problem arose or it will prevent you from making an error. Thinking your way through the problem like this will result in the success of any action you take. Anyone who masters that secret will rise high and reach every state that mortals can desire.

To be a knowledgeable,
successful person, see to it that
goodness is an established attribute
of character rather than an
accidental and isolated
occurrence.

True goodness means that your intentions are always beneficial, never hurtful. To maintain your beneficial intentions, it is necessary to renew your determination every day to follow the path of the knowledgeable, successful person and to always work to improve your character. For persevering in your efforts, you will find within yourself a wellspring of joy that will refresh and renew you all of your days. Good fortune and success will follow as closely as does your shadow in the full light of the sun.

*In cultivating oneself,
it is best to root out bad habits
and tolerate those that
are harmless.*

If you are too weak to overcome habits that are obviously bad for you, your future is indeed bleak. While temporary pleasures may accompany bad habits, they are, in the long run, detrimental. Even in the short run, they weaken you. Acquiring a long-run problem in exchange for a short-run pleasure is a poor bargain. It takes strength and determination to rid yourself of bad habits, but by so doing you gain control, increase your strength, and have a supremely better life. A knowledgeable, successful person is always in control of his habits. To be successful in rooting out bad habits, it is, however, wise to tolerate less harmful habits for a time; for if you are too strict with yourself, you may fail in your purpose.

*To act on the
spur of every whim
ultimately leads to
humiliation.*

What the heart desires, we tend to run after without a moment's hesitation, but there are three restraints to consider before acting or reacting that can free you from unwanted ties to people or events. First, do not run after all those you would like to influence. Instead, hold back if it is unseemly to make an approach. Second, do not yield to every whim of those who are engaging you in their service. Third, where the moods of the heart are concerned, do not ignore the possibility of holding back, for this is the basis of human freedom. Even in the face of desires that may strongly pull you, develop the strength to choose the wise course of action. This can be difficult, but it is essential if you are to be in charge of your fate, and such restraint leads to the attainment of goals and avoidance of ill fortune.

To enjoy a meaningful
way of life and to produce
long-lasting effects, the ability
to endure must be firmly
established within you.

To endure means to continue to the end—to continue in the face of obstacles, pain, fatigue, frustration, opposition, or hardship. Duration is a state that is not worn down by anything. When you have established the quality of endurance within yourself, you can reach any goal, overcome any obstacle, and bear any condition. Once established, that inner law of your being then determines all of your actions and leads to extraordinary well-being and abundant success. Gaining mastery of that one secret allows you to completely depend upon yourself to persevere until your goals are reached.

To be successful,
do not be rigid and immobile
in your thinking, but always
keep abreast of the time
and change with it.

The Universal law that provides for constant change is the only thing that does not change. To remain inflexible when all else is changing is to invite disaster. It is essential to your success that you set a firm course and that you be stable enough in your character not to waver with every passing fad. It is equally essential that you be aware of changing conditions and be open and flexible enough in your thinking to change with changing conditions. Maintaining rigidity leads to failure; remaining flexible leads to success.

*If you attempt
too much, you will
end by succeeding
in nothing.*

It is commendable to push yourself to new heights. In addition to the reward of reaching your goals, achieving your goals brings satisfaction and other benefits. If, however, you strive to reach unrealistic or unattainable goals, you court disaster and failure, and you may lose even that which you already have. The knowledgeable, successful person does not overreach himself or strive foolishly. In that way, he enjoys a lifetime of success. It is good to know when a task is too monumental and to back away. He who takes every turn is not wise.

SECRET 29

*To remain at the
mercy of moods of
hope and fear will cost you
your inner composure
and consistency.*

Hope contains the subtle fear that what you hope for will not come to pass. Fear contains the subtle hope that what you fear will not come to pass. Neither state is appropriate to the knowledgeable, successful person, who knows that everything that occurs is for his benefit and therefore turns everything fate brings to his advantage. To remain at the mercy of hope and fear is to bob like a cork on the ocean, your emotions rising and falling as your hopes and fears assail you. Living the life of the knowledgeable person is certain to secure your fate and bring you supreme success and good fortune. Therefore, have courage and faith and be joyous and all will be well. You are far more powerful than you suspect, and the Universal plan includes your well-being.

*If you live in a
state of perpetual hurry,
you will fail to attain
inner composure.*

Inner composure means having a settled state of mind—having calmness and tranquility. Whoever attains that most desirable state is then able to act without stress and therefore makes no mistakes. Constant hurrying wears you down, destroys your calmness, and puts lines in your face. Perpetual hurrying upsets your inner composure as well as your good judgment. By slowing down and nurturing yourself with the ways of the knowledgeable, successful person, you will achieve all else through the process of natural law.

When confronted with
insurmountable forces,
retreat is proper.

If you persist in fighting a battle that is beyond your capabilities, you risk depleting your resources so greatly that you cannot recover. To retreat does not mean to give up. On the contrary, retreating preserves resources and allows you time to regain your strength, renew your forces, and make new plans. Retreat then creates the opportunity for a countermovement, which will make possible your future success.

*Waiting should not
be mere empty hoping;
it should be filled with
the inner certainty of
reaching your goals.*

Everything changes and transforms. While you are waiting for a situation to transform itself, if you are uncertain about reaching your goals, your waiting will be filled with worrying and fearful imaginings, both of which are detrimental to productivity and lead away from success. If, instead, you are certain of reaching your goals, your waiting will be filled with happy thoughts and useful occupation, both of which lead directly to success.

The knowledgeable person is never led into baseness or vulgarity in a community of interests with people of low character.

You sometimes find yourself associating with inferior people because of the need to achieve a common goal. In their company, you may be tempted to pleasures and actions that are inappropriate for the knowledgeable, successful person. To participate in such low pleasures or actions would certainly bring remorse. Just as you should not allow yourself to be swept along by unfavorable circumstances without resisting, neither should you allow inferior people to erode your good character. By your determination to continue in what you know to be right, you will overcome even the greatest of adversities, and success and good fortune will naturally come to you.

*In financial matters,
well-being prevails when
expenditures and income
are in proportion.*

Out of debt, out of danger. You must not spend more than you have. Credit enslaves. Since all periods of prosperity are followed by periods of decline, the knowledgeable, successful person prepares for the times of decline during the times of prosperity. If you always spend all that you have, you will be unprepared in times of emergency. Such poor planning leads to the destruction of well-being and invites disaster. Whoever masters this one secret will live a life of such great abundance that from the excess he will be able to experience the joy of giving.

*Do not
be ashamed
of simplicity or
small means.*

Simplicity is the hallmark of the knowledgeable, successful person, while ostentation, or showing off, is the hallmark of the inferior person. There is no need to present false appearances. Even with slender means or no means at all, you can express the sentiments of your heart. In reality, you are appreciated not for the monetary value of your gifts but for the sentiments with which you give them. Making a show of what you have never endears you to your friends and neighbors.

*A compromise with evil
is not possible.*

To end a conflict with evil-minded people, you are sometimes tempted to compromise what you know to be right. Such compromising is an error, for evil must be completely eradicated if it is not to spring up again. The best way to overcome evil is to hold completely to what is good. To digress even slightly from that path is to start on the path of the inferior and unsuccessful person. To continue on that path can only lead to unfortunate results.

SECRET 37

In the time of gathering together,
you should make no arbitrary
choice of your associates.
There are secret forces at work,
bringing together those
who belong together.

An arbitrary choice is one that is made on the basis of personal preference, without regard to laws or principles. In the time of gathering together, the secret forces that are bringing together those who belong together may bring you into association with people who are not of your personal preference but who, nonetheless, may be of great benefit to you. The secret, therefore, counsels you in two ways: one, you should remain open-minded, and, two, you need not concern yourself about finding the right people. The Universe, which is fully aware of you, knows what and who you need for your growth and for your success.

*You must not
allow yourself
to be led astray
by a leader.*

Protecting yourself from being led astray does not mean that you should ignore a leader or ignore good counsel from a qualified person. You should, however, question whether a leader's course is best or honorable for you and then make your own decision about which course to take. Always be alert for that little inner voice each of us possesses, for it will prompt you to take the right course of action.

*The thoughts you hold
in your mind later manifest
in your physical body.*

The mind is a creator, and what you hold there manifests itself in one way or another. If you hold worrying and stress in your mind, they will manifest themselves in your body as tension and pain. If you hold thankfulness and joy in your mind, they will manifest themselves in your body as radiant health and a shining, happy face. The use of this one secret can magically transform your life, bringing you great joy, serenity, and happiness to spare.

Only when you go
to meet your fate resolutely
will you be equipped to
deal with it adequately.

To meet fate resolutely means that you have the determination to overcome whatever fate may bring, that you will not succumb to folly or temptation, and that you will not be turned aside from your chosen course. Only strong and courageous people can stand up to their fate, overcoming all obstacles. Their fierce determination enables them to endure to the end. With strength or courage, you can face things exactly as they are, without any sort of self-deception or illusion. When you have that attitude, a light develops out of events whereby you can recognize the path to success. By making that strong commitment, you actually cause favorable events to occur that would otherwise not have occurred. A person capable of this kind of commitment can reach any goal, overcome any obstacle, and fulfill any plan.

Slander will be silenced
if you do not gratify it
with injured retorts.

You can spend a lifetime tracking down and defending yourself against the negative things people say. It is better to simply go on with your own affairs. With nothing to keep the talk alive, it will die for lack of attention. The best defense against slander is to live the life of the knowledgeable, successful person, letting your actions and conduct speak for you.

On the road to success,
as you near the attainment of
your goal, you must beware
of becoming intoxicated
with your achievement.

If you allow yourself to become overly excited about an approaching success, you may become careless or light-headed and fail to pay attention to crucial matters, thereby ruining your success. It is precisely at the point of success that you must remain sober and cautious. By maintaining the same attitude and course of action that brought you to the point of success, you will surely and safely achieve your success.

SECRET 43

*If you neglect your
good qualities and virtues,
you will cease to be of value
to your friends and neighbors.
Soon, no one will seek you
out or bother about you.*

By nurturing your good qualities and virtues, you ensure that your inner worth will be inexhaustible, and all will seek you out. Like a spring of sparkling, clear water, no matter how much is drawn from you, more will remain and the greater your wealth will become. Those who understand these words will find them more precious than diamonds and gold.

You can succeed in life,
no matter your circumstances,
provided you have determination
and endurance and follow the
path of the knowledgeable,
successful person.

Whatever you now do, whatever you now believe, whatever your current circumstances may be, you are perfectly equipped and fully capable of fulfilling your needs and desires. The opportunities to achieve success are endless, and even those who start with nothing can succeed. But even the finest opportunity in the wrong hands comes to nothing. All that is necessary for you to achieve success, great success, is to cultivate endurance as an established trait of character, have determination to reach your goals, and follow the path of the knowledgeable, successful person. By accomplishing that, you will speed to your success as an eagle in flight.

In order to achieve a quiet heart,
rest and movement must follow
each other in accordance with
the demands of the time.

A quiet heart, meaning a contented, peaceful heart, is among the greatest possessions you can have. Achieving a quiet heart allows you to be sensitive to the subtle promptings from the world around you, which in turn allows you to move through life effortlessly and smoothly rather than with great effort and blundering. Acting in accord with the demands of the time produces harmony. If, however, you are still when the time for action comes, you will miss your opportunity, and what would have been easy to achieve becomes difficult. Or if you are in motion when the time for rest is at hand, you will be unprepared when the time for action comes. The knowledgeable, successful person first achieves a quiet heart and then acts. Whoever acts from these deep levels makes no mistakes.

In exercises in meditation and concentration, trying to force results will lead to an unwholesome outcome.

Trying to obtain by force what can only be obtained by relaxation and calmness will produce results opposite from the ones you hope to achieve. By first achieving inner composure, you can develop meditation and concentration naturally, thereby producing the desired result. Meditation and concentration are valuable tools. Meditation, a quieting of the mind and a cessation of thoughts, allows you to receive input from the subtle levels of the Universe. Concentration, a focusing of your thoughts, permits you to plan successfully. By learning to meditate and concentrate, your successful future is assured.

The knowledgeable, successful
person spends a lifetime
developing strong character,
and so enjoys a lifetime of
supreme good fortune
and great success.

A tree on a mountain develops slowly, according to the law of its being, and consequently stands firmly rooted. So also the development of one's character must undergo gradual development if it is to have a broad, stable base. The very gradualness of the development makes it necessary, however, to have perseverance lest slow progress become stagnation. For being successful in your efforts, you will also enjoy a lifetime of supreme good fortune and great success.

The knowledgeable person sees
and understands the transitory,
that which is temporary,
in the light of eternity.

You may imagine an endless future stretching out ahead of you and an endless past stretching out behind. You may believe that where you exist is the moment called now, the moment you may believe to be a tiny hairline that separates the future from the past. The reverse is true; all there is and was and ever will be is an endless now. Is it not always now? The knowledgeable person understands that this moment called now is all that exists and that every moment is therefore as much a part of eternity as eternity itself. He also understands that whatever occurs within this moment of now is perfect, just as eternity is perfect. Carrying his thought further, he understands that because he is part of eternity, he is perfect—and you are perfect. Anyone who completely grasps that concept will feel his sense of impermanence evaporating as mist in the air.

*If you would have
your relationship endure,
fix your mind on an end
that endures.*

All relationships run the danger of misunderstandings and disagreements arising that can cause a parting of the ways. If you permit yourself to drift along without having in mind the fixed goal of the continuation of your relationship, you may find that it continues or not, as the day may determine. By making a commitment to permanently maintain your relationship, you will set a standard against which you will measure all of the actions and decisions affecting your relationship. Having made that commitment, you will avoid the pitfalls and reefs that confront close relationships. By successfully putting this secret into action, you will be blessed with long-lasting friendships and beautiful, rewarding, soul-satisfying relationships.

Mad pursuit of pleasure
never takes one to the
goal of happiness.

No matter what your goals are, if you examine your motives in choosing them, you will discover that you have chosen your goals, one and all, because you believe that they will bring you happiness. Those who seek happiness through the mad pursuit of pleasure experience only temporary sensory enjoyment; they never arrive at their goals of true happiness. Following the path of the knowledgeable, successful person produces happiness, leads to happiness, and maintains happiness—deep down, soul-drenching happiness.

*Power best
expresses itself
in gentleness.*

The bully, the despot, and the person in authority who uses his power to hurt others are all universally disliked. They create the unpleasant environment within which they must exist. By contrast, the knowledgeable, successful person in a position of power can be clearly recognized by his gentleness. His gentle expression of power does not provoke resentment or incur resistance and so makes the attainment of his purposes and the continued growth of his power easy. By following the example of the knowledgeable, successful person, you will go your way unopposed on a smooth, easy road.

Even with just a small bit
of power, you can achieve
great success if you use
that power correctly.

To use a small amount of power correctly, first fix your goal firmly in your mind, seeing it clearly. Then, imagine yourself attaining it. Next, commit yourself to reaching the goal. Last, always use whatever power you have to move in the direction of attainment, taking every opportunity that comes along and turning it to your advantage. Your perseverance must never slacken. It is key that you do not allow opposing thoughts to dwell in your mind. Just as dripping water wears away even the hardest rock, you will eventually arrive at your goal. To accomplish a great goal with only a small amount of power is a wonderful accomplishment. It will bring you great respect and allow the power you have to blossom so that you will be able to accomplish other, greater deeds.

After a matter
has been thoroughly
considered, it is essential
to form a decision
and to act.

Reflection or pondering must not be carried too far, lest either cripple the power of decision. When the time for action has come, the moment must be seized. Once a matter has been thoroughly considered, anxious hesitation is a mistake that is bound to bring disaster because you will have missed your opportunity.

*Knowledge
is the key to
freedom.*

Knowing how to earn a living frees you from poverty. Knowing how to keep healthy frees you from sickness. Knowing how to entertain yourself frees you from boredom. Knowing the path of the knowledgeable, successful person frees you from misfortune, failure, and suffering.

Through hardness and selfishness, your heart grows rigid, and this rigidity leads to separation from others.

When you see someone in need and turn away from him, that is the beginning of hardness. When someone asks you for help and you refuse, selfishly hoarding what you have, the hardness grows. When someone asks you for forgiveness and you refuse, that is the beginning of rigidity. Soon you begin to look at everyone from behind a mask of hardness. That is your protection against their plea for help. Your voice becomes sharp and your manner truculent. Everyone avoids you except the hangers-on who are after the few crumbs that fall from your table. Hardness and selfishness are characteristics of the inferior person. Gentleness and generosity are characteristics of the superior person. Hardness and selfishness, gentleness and generosity—each bring their own inevitable results.

Unlimited possibilities
are not suited to mankind.
If they existed, our lives
would only dissolve
into the boundless.

Who is it that could choose among unlimited possibilities? Just to consider them would take all of eternity. Limitations are troublesome, but they are effective. The knowledgeable, successful person sets limits within which he experiences total freedom. In so doing, he achieves focus and success and avoids danger. When you come to know the secret of limitation, you will have avoided one of the most dangerous pitfalls to achieving your goals, and you will rise to dizzying heights of success.

*Through words and deeds
the knowledgeable person
moves heaven and earth.*

By your words and deeds you create good fortune and misfortune. Therefore, shouldn't you be careful of what you say and do? All words and deeds spring from within. If your heart is pure and your motivations that of the knowledgeable, successful person, your words will be direct and powerful and your actions will produce far-reaching, beneficial effects. If your heart is not as it should be, can anything else happen but that you fall into a pit of your own creation?

*If you depend on your
relationships for your happiness,
you will either be happy or sad
as your relationships
rise and fall.*

D o not make the mistake of relying on your mate, friends, and relatives for your happiness. Wed your happiness to that which endures: the path of the knowledgeable, successful person. A quiet, self-contained joy, desiring nothing from without and resting content with everything, allows you to remain independent and free—free in the quiet security of a heart fortified within itself.

Exceptional modesty and conscientiousness are sure to be rewarded with great success and good fortune.

Being modest means that you have cultivated a humble attitude and you do not give yourself airs or strut about trying to impress people; nor are you boastful of your accomplishments. Being conscientious means that you fulfill your tasks and obligations with great care. If you hold a high position and are exceptionally modest and conscientious, your radiance will be like the sun at midday, and no blame or resentment will attach to your progress. The attainment of your goals will be rapid and easy. If you hold a low position and are exceptionally modest and conscientious, you will be recognized and rewarded, and you will rise quickly through the ranks.

SECRET 60

*The knowledgeable, successful
person is reverent, at all times
acknowledging the great Creator
and the wondrousness
of the Universe.*

When you see a great painting, you acknowledge the painter. When you see a great structure, you acknowledge the builder. When you see the Universe, that tiny portion of it that is visible to you, how can you fail to acknowledge its Creator? When great grief, misfortune, or illness befalls you and no human can help, you instinctively turn to the divine for help. That is only natural since each of us inherently knows the truth of our existence and origin. None of us can fathom how this Universe of ours began, nor can any of us foretell when it will end. Not one of us can even say why it or we exist. Since we can only wonder at it all, does it not seem immensely egotistical and foolish not to be reverent in the face of that awesomeness?

The knowledgeable, successful person is completely sincere in his thoughts and actions.

In sorrow and reverence, your feelings should mean more to you than ceremoniousness, which is primarily for the benefit of others. In personal expenditures, you should place the highest value on thrift. In conduct, your actions should be simple and unpretentious. Neither should you pretend love and other emotions that you do not feel. Like all false illusions, they only bring hurt and despair in their train and bode ill for the perpetrator. There is no need to pretend or deceive. You need only fix your eyes on the path of the knowledgeable, successful person, be truly yourself, and all else will be accomplished as a result of natural law.

*It is only after
perfect balance has
been achieved that any
misstep brings
imbalance.*

It is only after the achievement of success, wealth, fame, happiness, love, popularity, or possessions that you can be burdened with the fear of losing them. This is a caution that you are to remain modest and vigilant once you have acquired your treasure, whatever it is, or the same law that brought it to you will remove it from you or cause it to work to your detriment. You should not be deluded that your achievements and possessions are the end-all and be-all of life. They are merely the objects you have chosen to lead yourself along the path of life. It is the path itself that is the end-all and be-all, for on that path you shall learn the lessons of life and perfect yourself as a divine incarnation.

Even the

finest clothes

turn to rags.

Everything, the moment it is made, begins to decay. Is it wise, therefore, to set much store on finery and other such objects? The knowledgeable, successful person does not attach great importance to things that decay. Instead, he attaches great importance to things that endure: his integrity, his honor, his virtue, and his appreciation and reverence for All-That-Is. That is not to say that you should not value your possessions, for they can bring much pleasure. But you should not set great store by them; for possessions are transitory, and there are other, greater treasures.

There is no plain
not followed by a slope,
no increase not followed
by a decrease.

In our constantly changing Universe, the forces of light and dark, good and evil, prosperity and decline are ever alternating, the increase of one bringing a decrease in the other. It is an eternal law of the Universe that everything, when it reaches its maximum potential, turns toward its opposite. Knowing that law, the knowledgeable, successful person provides for a time of decrease in times of prosperity. He builds himself up during times of good health and so prepares against a time of illness. He takes precautions in times of safety that protect him in times of danger. He thinks ahead and, in so doing, is prepared. He thereby enjoys a lifetime of supreme good fortune and great success.

131

You should not complain,
but always enjoy and be grateful
for the good fortune
you still possess.

In an undesirable situation or when confronted with a loss, the inferior person bitterly complains and curses his luck. The knowledgeable, successful person remembers the good things still left to him and smiles. He knows that the seemingly undesirable situation or loss will ultimately be a benefit to him; thus, he responds in a positive way. The inferior person is sad; the superior person is glad. Each is in charge of his response. Each has set the pattern for the continuing course of events. If you master this one secret, you will find yourself always in the best possible situation, enjoying the wonders life holds for the enlightened.

*If you are not dazzled
by enticing goals and remain
true to yourself, you will travel
through life on a smooth
and level road.*

Great riches or enticements that dazzle you may also cause you to attempt to get them by inappropriate means. Such actions always lead to remorse. If you are true to yourself, if you live up to the best within yourself, you will walk the path of the knowledgeable, successful person. In so doing, you will reap the rewards of a prince and the glory of a king.

At the beginning of a project,
if many boastful claims are made,
the successful attainment
of the goal becomes far
more difficult.

When no claims are put forward, no resistance arises. By cultivating modesty, you will make swift, sure progress because no resentment will attach to you. If you remain modest despite your merit, you will be beloved and will win the support necessary to carry out even difficult and dangerous undertakings. When you make boastful claims, however, you jeopardize the attainment of your goals. Even if you are moderately successful but have fallen short of your claims, people will say that you failed. Knowing that one secret will make the attainment of your goals far easier.

Not a whole day.

This is a secret from the most ancient times. It means that when the knowledgeable, successful person perceives that action is required, he does not let even a day pass before taking the required action. Opportunity comes in a flash and sometimes disappears in a flash. When you see your opportunity before you, seize it and make it your own. In that way, you will not have to lament lost opportunities, and your success will blossom like wildflowers in a sunny meadow after a spring rain.

If you would rule,

you must first

learn to serve.

By first learning to serve, you will come to understand those who will eventually serve you. The only valid reason for a knowledgeable, successful person to want to rule is so he can better serve those he wishes to rule. If you are unprepared or unwilling to serve your followers, it is better for them, and for you, that you never achieve rulership, because if you do and then cease to serve them, you will lose your following. All your efforts will have been for naught and you will suffer great embarrassment. Only through serving can you obtain from those you rule the joyous assent that is necessary if they are to follow you.

*In friendships
and close relationships,
you must make a
careful choice.*

Certain people uplift you; others pull you down. Certain people give you strength; others drain your energy. You must choose your friends carefully. Good friends, like good neighbors, are an endless benefit. Bad relationships can ruin a lifetime. Following the path of the knowledgeable, successful person permits a natural selection that will find you only with the best-quality friends.

*If one clings
to the little boy,
one foregoes becoming
the strong man.*

If you are to become a strong, independent person, at some point in your life you must leave behind your childish ideas and your need to cling to someone else. If, as a parent, you pamper your children, you will prevent them from gaining strength on their own and from becoming strong and independent adults. If you always carry your children, they will never develop their own muscles to walk and run. Sometimes a generous, loving parent is the most difficult hurdle a developing child has to overcome. Similarly, at some point in your own life, you must leave behind all that holds you back—preconceived ideas, beliefs that do not benefit you, dependencies of every nature, and fear of the future. It takes courage, great courage, to live in that manner, but here is a secret within a secret: you have enough courage to overcome even your greatest fears. Fear and courage come into the world together. You only need to call upon your courage to overcome even your greatest fears.

SECRET 72

Every person must have

something to follow—

a lodestar.

We all need something to bring out the best in ourselves and provide direction for our development, such as the secrets in this book. By holding the image of the knowledgeable, successful person in your mind as your lodestar and keeping aware of the secrets, you will achieve not only supreme success but also great happiness, peace, and security.

In following the path of the
knowledgeable, successful person,
slight digressions from the good
cannot be avoided, but you must
turn back before going too far.

When you have turned onto the path of the inferior person—and we all do that at times—it is only natural that you will feel remorse, powerful remorse, but that is a good sign. However, do not carry remorse too far. After making whatever amends are necessary, you must continue on, resolving to be more cautious. To follow the path of the knowledgeable, successful person takes great courage, firm determination, and fierce perseverance. You must watch like a hungry hawk for transgressions, and if you find them, you must turn back immediately. This is an act of self-mastery and is highly commendable. Having turned back, you will progress like a hurricane, sweeping all obstacles from your path, and supreme good fortune and great success will quickly follow.

If you are not as you should be,
you will have misfortune,
and it does not further you
to undertake anything.

The path of the inferior person is filled with pitfalls of his own making. In any plan or undertaking that you conceive, there is only one constant: you. If your character is flawed, if you cannot depend upon yourself to be efficient, careful, cautious, persevering, or honorable, you are a danger and a detriment to your own plans, and it will not profit you to undertake anything. If your character is without flaw, you can carry out even difficult and perilous undertakings without fear of failure.

*Only through daily
self-renewal of character
can you continue at the
height of your powers.*

It takes Herculean effort to reach the peak of perfection in any area of life and continuous effort to remain there. Every day you must expend some effort refreshing yourself with the ways of the knowledgeable, successful person. Reading great books, talking to like-minded people, teaching others, studying the deeds of ancient heroes, and thinking about your actions of the day to see whether you are being the best you can be are all ways to continue on the path to great success. As you grow in awareness, your power will grow and your attainments will be like the harvest after a perfect summer. There is no other activity that will reward you as richly as the daily self-renewing of your character.

SECRET 76

You have received
a nature that is innately good.
When your thoughts and actions
are in accord with your nature,
you will enjoy great good fortune
and supreme success.

You are a perfect being, a divine incarnation. Do not be deluded by outer appearances; you are always a perfect being. When, however, you act out of greed, selfishness, meanness, hatred, or other inferior motives, you act the part of a lesser being and will experience pain, despair, and frustration. Those feelings are not a punishment, although they seem so. They are there to let you know that you have departed from the path of the knowledgeable, successful person. Feelings of love and joy let you know that you are on the path. Whatever you are experiencing is a result of your intentions, your thoughts, and your actions. It is you who are in charge of your fate, not another.

*You should not set your eyes
on the harvest while planting it,
nor on the use of the ground
while clearing it.*

Every task must receive the attention it deserves if it is to turn out well. Anticipating the outcome of your efforts may cause you to become impatient and overeager, hurrying to complete your task. Hasty or careless work will result in unsatisfactory performance of your task, which, of course, will bring about an unsatisfactory result. You must do every task for its own sake, doing it as well as you can. When you live in this way, good fortune and great success are sure to be yours.

Words are movements
going from within, outward.
Eating and drinking are movements
that go from without, inward.
Both movements can be
modified by tranquility.

Tranquility means being calm and peaceful, experiencing a sense of well-being. Everything in its proper measure benefits you. The same thing carried to excess destroys you. The way to achieve tranquility is to follow the path of the knowledgeable, successful person, who is careful in his words and temperate in eating and drinking. Always, it is the excesses, too much or too little, that destroy you. Moderation will always find you enjoying the great rewards of life.

*Exceptional enterprises
cannot succeed unless the
utmost caution is observed
in their beginnings.*

In the beginning of even small things, exceptional care must be exercised if planting is to lead to flowering. How much more, then, should exceptional care be exercised when great or dangerous undertakings are begun? A flaw built into the beginning increases with time and, if not corrected, will ultimately cause the enterprise to fail. The knowledgeable, successful person can always see the end in the beginning. He knows the seeds and, exercising great care, enjoys a lifetime of success and good fortune.

SECRET 80

*Danger has
an important and
beneficial use.*

Being aware of danger causes you to take the necessary precautions that will protect you from harm when danger arises. By taking precautions, you have used danger to further the achievement of your success and you will protect what you already have.

SECRET 81

Every ending

contains a new

beginning.

All endings always and immediately produce the beginnings of something else. The path of the knowledgeable, successful person, which only leads to supreme good fortune and great success, is always directly in front of you. You may take the first step upon it at any time and magically transform your circumstances. Because of the Universal law of cause and effect, these benefits are available to everyone, withheld from no one. The path of the inferior person is also always directly in front of you, bringing its lessons of hardship, misery, and despair, but only so that you will ultimately come to know the truth. At each step of your way, you must always choose between those two paths. The beginning of one is always the ending of the other. Your future is entirely in your own hands, and everything is possible.

Knowing these secrets will keep you safe from harm and lead you to great good fortune. May you soar to the skies of success as though on the wings of six dragons!

Chris

Other Titles by Power Press

Available from your favorite neighborhood and online bookstores:

Zen and the Art of Happiness
By Chris Prentiss, Trade Paperback, $10.95; Hardback, $14.95

The Alcoholism and Addiction Cure:
A Holistic Approach to Total Recovery
By Chris Prentiss, Trade Paperback, $15.95; 10-CD Audio, $39.95

Be Who You Want, Have What You Want: Change Your
Thinking, Change Your Life
By Chris Prentiss, Trade Paperback, $15.95

The I Ching: The Book of Answers, New Revised Edition
By Wu Wei, Trade Paperback, $15.95

A Tale of the I Ching: How the Book of Changes Began
By Wu Wei, Trade Paperback, $10.95

I Ching Wisdom: Guidance from the Book of Answers, Vol. I
By Wu Wei, Trade Paperback, $12.95

I Ching Wisdom: More Guidance from the Book of Answers, Vol. II
By Wu Wei, Trade Paperback, $12.95

I Ching Readings: Interpreting the Answers
By Wu Wei, Trade Paperback, $14.95

I Ching Life: Becoming Your Authentic Self
By Wu Wei, Trade Paperback, $12.95

I Ching Workbook
The entire text of *The I Ching: The Book of Answers* and 100 workbook
pages to record your answers
By Wu Wei, Trade Paperback, $19.95

I Ching Workbook Deluxe Gift Set
The entire text of *The I Ching: The Book of Answers* and 100 workbook
pages to record your answers, 10" yarrow stalks, sandalwood incense,
Auroshikha incense holder, and silk I Ching cloth
By Wu Wei, $27.95

I Ching Gift Set
The entire text of *The I Ching: The Book of Answers* and 7" yarrow stalks
By Wu Wei, $19.95

50 Yarrow Stalks from China
Handpicked by farmers in northeast China specifically for use with the
I Ching. 7" yarrow stalks (50), $10.95; 10" yarrow stalks (50), $12.95

Published by Power Press
www.PowerPressPublishing.com

Bookstores, please contact SCB Distributors toll free at
800-729-6423 or 310-532-9400. Fax: 310-532-7001
E-mail: info@scbdistributors.com
Website: www.scbdistributors.com

For foreign and translation rights, contact Nigel J. Yorwerth
E-mail: Nigel@PublishingCoaches.com

CHRIS PRENTISS is the cofounder and codirector, along with his son Pax, of the world-famous Passages Addiction Cure Center in Malibu, California. He is also the author of the popular *Zen and the Art of Happiness*, *The Alcoholism and Addiction Cure: A Holistic Approach to Total Recovery*, and *Be Who You Want, Have What You Want*. He has written a dozen books on Chinese philosophy and personal growth under his pen name, Wu Wei. Prentiss has also led personal empowerment workshops in Southern California and has written, produced, and directed a feature film. He resides with his wife, Lyn, in Malibu, California.